FANTASTIC BEASTS
AND WHERE TO FIND THEM

FASHION SKETCHBOOK

· J.K. ROWLING'S ·
WW
· WIZARDING WORLD ·

SCHOLASTIC LTD.

www.fantasticbeasts.co.uk

Scholastic Children's Books
Euston House, 24 Eversholt Street,
London NW1 1DB, UK

A division of Scholastic Ltd
London ~ New York ~ Toronto ~ Sydney ~ Auckland
Mexico City ~ New Delhi ~ Hong Kong

First published in the US by Scholastic Inc, 2016
Published in the UK by Scholastic Ltd, 2016

Book Design by Erin McMahon
Illustrations by Miss Led and Lauren Mortimer

ISBN 978 1407 17344 3

Printed and bound in Germany

2 4 6 8 10 9 7 5 3 1

FANTASTIC BEASTS
AND WHERE TO FIND THEM

FASHION SKETCHBOOK

INTRODUCTION

Newt Scamander, the world's pre-eminent Magizoologist, strongly believes that magical creatures should be studied and protected. Newt has made this his life's mission, travelling the globe to carry out his research.

The adventure begins when Newt arrives in New York City in the winter of 1926, with nothing more in his possession than the clothes on his back and one modest leather case. But his is no ordinary case – it is also the home of a fantastic array of magical creatures.

Jacob Kowalski – who is referred to by the American wizarding community as a No-Maj because he does not have magical powers – meets Newt when they are both at a local bank. Following a misunderstanding, Jacob and Newt get into a skirmish outside the bank, and the two accidentally switch cases. Jacob gets the surprise of his life when he returns home and opens Newt's case, unwittingly unleashing many of the Magizoologist's beloved beasts.

Meanwhile, there is something dark and ferocious terrorizing New York City. It's crushing cars, blasting through walls and shattering windows. Some No-Majs explain the unusual disturbances as strange weather, but others suspect the truth: magic is afoot. Mary Lou Barebone, the leader of the New Salem Philanthropic Society, leads a vocal charge in alerting people about what she believes is sinister witchcraft and wizardry all around them.

As Newt searches the city for his escaped creatures, he becomes further entangled not only with Jacob, but also with two witch sisters named Tina and Queenie Goldstein, who work for the Magical Congress of the United States of America, MACUSA. Once MACUSA becomes aware of Newt's escaped creatures, they blame him for the troubles in the city.

How can Newt save himself – and his creatures – if no one will listen to the truth?

NEWT SCAMANDER

is the world's pre-eminent Magizoologist. He wears practical clothing because he always needs to be ready to go on an adventure to learn about and protect the magical creatures of the wizarding world.

Colour and embellish Newt's outfit.

If you could design some outfits for Newt, what would they look like?

TINA GOLDSTEIN

works for the Magical Congress of the United States of America, known as MACUSA. She dresses in simple and comfortable clothing that makes it easy for her to blend into crowds of No-Majs and conduct investigations.

Colour and embellish Tina's outfit.

What sort of outfits would you design for Tina?

QUEENIE GOLDSTEIN

is a glamorous and fashion-forward witch living in New York City. She and Tina are sisters.

Colour and embellish Queenie's outfit.

Queenie likes to keep up with the latest trends!
What sort of stylish outfits would you design for her?

JACOB KOWALSKI

has dreams of opening his own bakery, but first he needs to get a loan from the bank. For his important meeting with the bank manager, he dresses in a three-piece suit. The suit includes a jacket, waistcoat and trousers.

Colour and embellish Jacob's outfit.

Design some outfits that you think would look
good if you were headed to an important meeting.

Jacob wears a dark red tie with his suit.
Create and colour your own patterns on the ties below.

MILDRED is Jacob's fiancée. But when she finds out Jacob did not get the bank loan, she gives him back her engagement ring. Her cheery pink outfit is a sad contrast to her and Jacob's state of affairs.

Colour and embellish Mildred's outfit.

Design your own
outfits for Mildred.

One of Newt's beasts, a Niffler, is attracted to all the shiny and
sparkly rings and bracelets in jewellery shop windows.

Craft your own ring and bracelet designs below. Would your jewellery attract the Niffler?

Tina and Queenie share a stylish apartment adorned with quaint decor and colourful wallpaper patterns. In their living room, Queenie keeps a dressmaker's dummy that she uses to create her own fashions using her wand.

It's your turn! Design your own fashions on
the dressmaker's dummies below.

Queenie uses lots of different materials and
colourful fabrics in her dressmaking.

Design your own patterns on the swatches of fabric below.

Witches have magical products that they use to help
make everyday life easier – and more beautiful.

Design and colour your own bottles and jars below.

Create a soft daytime look on Queenie by drawing light make-up below.

Create a dynamic night-time look on Queenie by drawing dark make-up above.

Design your own winter fashions on the models below.

Design your own party fashions on the models below.

Colour and embellish these women's
shoe styles from the 1920s.

Queenie's short curls are
high style for the time period.
Create and colour your own hairstyles below.

TINA makes Newt and Jacob stay at her apartment so they don't get into any more trouble on the streets of New York. That night, she wears light blue pyjamas with a floral pattern to bed.

Colour and embellish Tina's pyjamas.

Design your own pyjamas for Tina.

QUEENIE even looks fashionable at bedtime! She sleeps in a pink nightdress with white lace trim. A silky pink robe finishes off her look.

Colour and embellish Queenie's pyjamas.

Design your own
pyjamas for Queenie.

Design your own chic city fashions on the models below.

Design your own summer fashions on the models below.

The
AMERICAN
Charmer

August 1926
23 Shrinks

SPELLBINDING
SUMMER SIZZLERS!
Latest Cuts Straight from the Catwalk

SERAPHINA PICQUERY

is the President of MACUSA. When an assembly
is in session, she wears a sleek black robe and a
matching golden headpiece.

Colour and embellish Seraphina's outfit.

Design your own outfits for Seraphina.

Finger waves were a very popular
hairstyle for women in the 1920s.
Create and colour your own hairstyles below.

PERCIVAL GRAVES

is Director of Magical Security at MACUSA. He always dresses to impress, and his commanding black clothing matches his authoritative presence.

Colour and embellish Graves's suit.

Design your own suits for Graves.

Design and colour your own patterns on the waistcoats below.

MARY LOU is the leader of

the New Salem Philanthropic Society. She hates witchcraft, and her stern philosophies match her dark clothing and severe appearance.

Colour and embellish Mary Lou's outfit.

Design your own outfits for Mary Lou.

CREDENCE, Mary

Lou's adopted son, wears dark, simple clothing that befits his role as a member of the New Salem Philanthropic Society.

Colour and embellish Credence's suit.

Design your own suits for Credence.

CHASTITY also participates in her adoptive mother's society and wears basic, unadorned clothing, like her older brother, Credence.

Colour and embellish Chastity's dress.

Design your own outfits for Chastity.

MODESTY, the youngest adopted daughter of Mary Lou, wears drab grey clothing. The only embellishment on her garment is a cluster of embroidered flowers, which are hardly cheery.

Colour and embellish Modesty's outfit.

Design your own outfits for Modesty.

Colour and embellish these men's hat styles from the 1920s.

D raw your own hats below.

HENRY SHAW JR

is a politician running for re-election to the United States Senate. He makes sure his clothing is always starched and pressed to give him a polished public appearance.

Colour and embellish Henry Jr's outfit.

Design your own outfits for Henry Jr.

Colour and embellish these men's shoe styles from the 1920s.

LANGDON SHAW is

a member of the prominent Shaw family, but his influence does not extend beyond the family name. He doesn't wear the same refined clothing of his brother and father, instead favouring more simple suits.

Colour and embellish Langdon's outfit.

Design your own outfits for Langdon.

QUEENIE always makes sure that her outfit is perfectly accessorized. When it's cold outside, she wears a pink coat with an oversized velvet collar and matching hat.

Colour and embellish Queenie's outfit.

Design your own outfits for Queenie.

Colour and embellish these women's hat styles from the 1920s.

Draw your own hats above.

Design your own fashions for a big
night out on the models below.

Design your own fashions for a big night
out on the models below.

During the 1920s, many women styled their
hair with one curl on their face,
known as a kiss curl.
Create and colour your own hairstyles below.

Jewellery from the 1920s often incorporated trends from the time period, such as geometric designs and patterns.

Design your own necklaces on the stands below.

Necklines during the 1920s were often very ornate, with lots of beads, sequins and straps.

Design your own detailed neckline
on the model below.

Add hair accessories like hair clips, pins and headbands to the styles below.

Every witch and wizard needs his or her own wand to cast magic spells.

Draw your own wand below.

Design an outfit inspired by the Occamy.

THE OCCAMY

is a plumed serpent with lustrous, iridescent feathers. Its two large wings are reminiscent of a dragon.

Design an outfit inspired
by the Billywig.

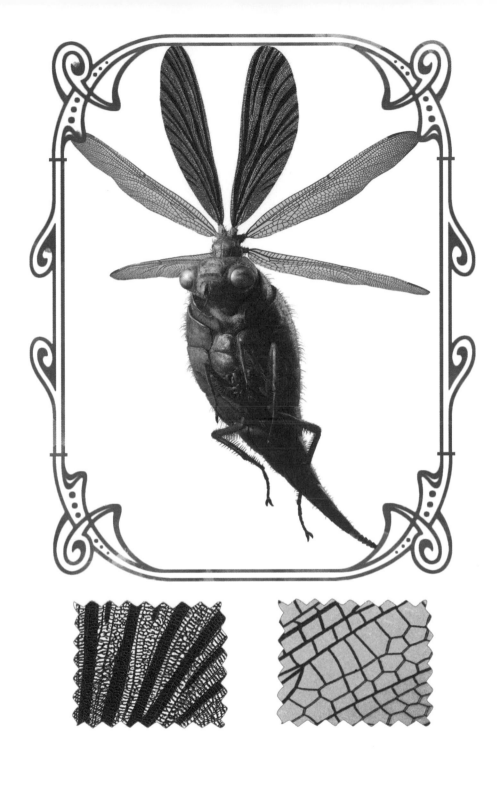

THE BILLYWIG has

a body that is a deep and brilliant

blue, the colour of sapphires.

Design an outfit inspired
by the Doxy.

THE DOXY has bulbous compound eyes and the scaly skin of a lizard that changes colours to fit its mood or environment. Long, multicoloured ears fan out from its head.

Design an outfit inspired by the Niffler.

THE NIFFLER has bright, beady eyes, dark fur and a duck-like, flesh-coloured bill like a platypus.

Design an outfit inspired
by the Demiguise.

THE DEMIGUISE has long
silver-white hair and doleful brown eyes,
which give it the appearance of an old, wise
sage.

Design an outfit inspired by the Fwooper.

THE FWOOPER is a small bird-like beast with delicate purple feathers that can consume giant hunks of meat in one bite.

THE THUNDERBIRD is an eagle-like beast with six wings on its majestic body. It

arranges its multiple sets of feathers in such a way as to present dazzling images of the sun and sky.

THE SWOOPING EVIL has a spiked and scaly reptilian body, complete

with a skull-like head and fierce fangs. Its wings possess the vibrant blue colouration of a moth or butterfly.